Praise for
This Is Our Summons Now

These are passionate poems that insist on living-in-the-word and map the path of a speaker who will not be pigeon-holed into one singular category. *This Is Our Summons Now* is a spellbinding and memorable debut collection.

—**Sean Frederick Forbes**, author of *Providencia: A Book of Poems*

In his writing, R. Joseph Rodríguez always tugs on our hearts with his vulnerability mixed with power. His words are showered in love and heavy with pondering. We feel him, we hear him, and we understand him. These poems, therefore, humanize us a bit more. The titles alone are worth studying and the organization of each section is phenomenal. We want to remember, pronounce, understand the occupations, interrogate, and offer, as he calls us to do. These words should be read carefully and eaten with a hot chocolate on the side. What a treat to the soul and a blessing to every classroom that will use them!

—**Lorena E. Germán**, author of *Textured Teaching: A Framework for Culturally Sustaining Practices*

R. Joseph Rodríguez has given us poems, written in both English and Spanish, attentive to many of the cultural and social divisions that separate us from ourselves and from others. "I with my American entangled tongue and mashed mind/am endangered in this strange land," he writes. Recovering his history, using both of his languages, recalling his memories of creative forebears (especially mothers and grandmothers), embracing the education of his students, and unafraid to love, Rodríguez writes poems that variously explore how to make us see our essentially human and more humane selves. In a time of social and climate emergency, it is good to have these poems among us.

—**Margaret Gibson**, Poet Laureate of the State of Connecticut

R. Joseph Rodríguez's maiden collection of poems summons the reader to witness the poet's responses to a multitude of borders and margins lived in his native Texas (indeed a state of contested borders and margins) and in the world that justifies the urgency of now. Nonetheless, there is kindness and compassion and generosity in the summons. It is both a summons and a gift.

—**Rafael Jesús González**, Poet Laureate, Berkeley, California

The energy in these poems, both on the surface and behind the words and lines, in both español and English, is buoyant. Each poem carries an optimism, a playfulness, small but very real joys, that will lift you up. Even in the poems speaking of dark experiences (domestic abuse, systemic racism, bullying, self-doubt), there is inextinguishable light, something generous that is and that will be. Take it with you after you read these poems, but never forget to share.

—**Crag Hill**, coeditor of *Level Land:*
Poems For and About the I35 Corridor

In this lyrical book, *This Is Our Summons Now: Poems*, R. Joseph Rodríguez invites us into his heart-home, where familia summons us to listen, to act, to respond—the ancestors, the abuelitas, the tias, the mother and father and siblings are all here, calling us to commune.

—**Guadalupe Garcia McCall**, Pura Belpré Award-winning
author of *Under the Mesquite*

These are the vigilant thoughts of a serious thinker. R. Joseph Rodríguez is a poet true to himself who insists on exposing the beauty, the anguish, and the complexity of his world. His vision is crisp; the emotion he portrays is raw and honest; and there is corazón in every word. Most importantly, Rodríguez's book reminds us that poetry is for everyone, both for the poetically practiced and for novices unaccustomed to the intense power of words on the page; his poetry is for anyone who craves insight into the beauty of our shared realities.

—**Ignacio Martínez**, author of *The Intimate Frontier:*
Friendship and Civil Society in Northern New Spain

Essential, elegant, earthen, transcendent, respectful, tender, rich with care—the poems of R. Joseph Rodríguez lift us everywhere, and they have since he was very young. This gleaming book is cause for great celebration!

—**Naomi Shihab Nye**, Young People's Poet Laureate, The Poetry Foundation

This hauntingly beautiful collection of poems pulls the reader in completely—mind, body, and spirit. *This is Our Summons Now: Poems* invites us to do the honest work of facing our complicated histories and ourselves. The book calls for our liberation, if only we can summon the courage to listen.

—**Yolanda Sealey-Ruiz**, author of *Love from the Vortex & Other Poems* and *The Peace Chronicles*

This Is Our Summons Now: Poems

FLOWERSONG
P R E S S

poems by
R. Joseph Rodríguez

FlowerSong Press
Copyright © 2022 by R. Joseph Rodríguez
ISBN: 978-1-953447-62-3
Library of Congress Control Number: 2022933303

Published by FlowerSong Press
in the United States of America.
www.flowersongpress.com

Cover Art: *Los Paseños* by Joel Salcido © 2020. All rights reserved.
www.joelsalcido.com

Author Photo Credit: Philip Goetz, 2021

Cover Design by Priscilla Celina Suarez

Set in Adobe Garamond Pro

NOTICE: SCHOOLS AND BUSINESSES
FlowerSong Press offers copies of this book at quantity discount with bulk
purchase for educational, business, or sales promotional use. For information,
please email the Publisher at info@flowersongpress.com.

Al pueblo del sol y nuestra multitud

To the people of the sun and our multitudes

CONTENTS

II.
Occupation

III.
Interrogation

IV.
Offerings

This Is Our Summons Now: Poems

Introduction
by Sean Frederick Forbes

The charm, intention, urgency, and wonder in the title *This Is Our Summons Now* points to the power and talent of R. Joseph Rodríguez as a poet. It's a title that invokes a myriad of provocative feelings and reactions. The word "summons" is direct, formal, and official, since its most common meaning is that one must appear before a judge in a court of law. In a school or work setting, it means one must appear before a principal or supervisor. In both instances, one might become anxious and uneasy, since there's a feeling of impending doom followed by a penalty and/or reprimand. Also, one can "summons" for medical assistance, one can "summons" a meeting of advisors, and one can manage to "summons" a smile in an awkward situation. Moreover, art, education, literature, music, nature, religion, and spirituality all have the alluring power to "summons" a person's inner core at any given moment; an experience of awe and ecstasy; a calling.

In the narrative arc presented in *This Is Our Summons Now*, a reader encounters and engages with 67 poems written in various poetic forms and styles, the English and Spanish languages, historical figures that have been obscured only to then be resurrected by an earnest and generous speaker, and there's a sense of voice that is indicative of Rodríguez's many noble roles as educator, scholar, poet, interpreter, and writer. In this collection, one will find personal poems that strike with resounding social significance from a speaker who identifies as gay, of Mexican origin, and was born and raised in Texas, as well as poems that survey a sometimes gentle and sometimes violent historical landscape with visceral intimacy.

The first poem in the collection titled "Henrietta Lacks: HeLa" contains an anecdotal subtitle from the speaker, "*(after reading Skloot)*," which refers to the nonfiction book *The Immortal Life of Henrietta Lacks* (2010) written by American science writer Rebecca Skloot. The book focuses on Henrietta Lacks, the African American woman who, in 1951, underwent a biopsy of a cervical tumor, and unbeknownst to Lacks and her family, these cancer cells were extracted for the sake of medical observation and research. These cancer cells, known as the HeLa cell line, still remain in wide use in medical research today. In the first four lines of Rodríguez's poem, the speaker addresses Lacks directly stating: "Ethics / we learn / with your immortal / existence." The words in the poem are offered to Lacks with care, honor, and respect as befitting of a medical heroine. "Henrietta Lacks: HeLa" is a poem that extends another literary contribution in reverence to Lacks's life and story not having been discussed and widely known outside of the medical community prior to the publication of Skloot's book.

The speaker invites the reader to observe the desert landscape as being fecund, inspirational, lively, and wondrous. In the poem "at Sierra de los Mansos" the title refers to the original Spanish name of the Franklin Mountains in Texas that extend from El Paso del Norte into New Mexico. It's a mountain range known for biking, hiking, nature walks, and rock climbing. In the poem the speaker is hiking and as he looks around, he makes an emphatic statement in the first two lines: "nobody says the names / the given names by native peoples." The reader takes on the perspective of a speaker who pays homage to the countless borderlands histories, names, and narratives that have been marginalized and underconsidered and thus receive nominal attention in the development of American histories and identities. Rodríguez reveals to the reader the many ways in which one can resurrect and write these narratives and voices into being once again.

Rodríguez's ability to present poems in varying line and stanza lengths, as well as diverse poetic forms and styles, allows the reader to think about the way a poem looks on the page. There are concrete poems, also known as visual poems, presented as a means to consider how language and image operate simultaneously on the page. In a poem such as "To Father," the reader immediately notices that the words are filled with mourning and with phrases such as "after the ICU" and "after the burial," yet in 13 lines the speaker presents the graceful and hopeful image of a bird in flight. "Everyjuan/x" is a short poem that dazzles the reader in that it's comprised of only 26 words and follows the sequence of the alphabet, while also creating a compelling linguistic narrative.

What's most memorable and impressionable in the collection is the way Rodríguez writes in both the English and Spanish languages. Some poem titles are written in Spanish while the poem itself is in English, other poems contain words and phrases in Spanish without footnotes, other poems are written entirely in Spanish without an accompanying translation, and some of the poems written entirely in English don't have Spanish translations as well. The reader becomes immersed in the speaker's distinctive bilingual, bicultural, and biliteracy experience. The two poems "In Memoriam" and "En memoria" are so linguistically heavy-hitting, because they convey the unspeakable loss of those who have died and continue to die from AIDS-related complications. Both the English and Spanish-language versions employ spare aesthetics in that they are both six lines long and highlight the ways in which both world languages mirror each other, since the Spanish acronym for AIDS is SIDA. What's offered to the reader is a clear, poignant, and solemn narrative that is emotionally, psychologically, and visually thought-provoking.

These are passionate poems that insist on living-in-the-word and map the path of a speaker who will not be pigeon-holed into one singular category. *This Is Our Summons Now* is a spellbinding and memorable debut collection, one that I will have the pleasure of reading and teaching in the classroom for many years.

Thompson, Connecticut
February 1, 2022

Author's Note

I fondly remember creativity appearing all around me since I was a young boy. In a sense, the creative mind was often summoned to create, design, and tell a story or for laborious affairs. For instance, I recall the artistic planning and deep thinking of my mother, grandmother, great-grandmother, aunts, and great-aunts in their baking, calculations, canning, cooking, crocheting, diaries, listings, notetaking, painting, planting, prayers, sewing, stitching, and writings that included their families and ancestors. Each year we witnessed the re-enactment of Mary and Joseph in their journey from Nazareth to Bethlehem and in their search for posada; each of us had a role. Also, my father, grandfathers, great-grandfather, and uncles used applied mathematics for budgets, construction, and mechanics. They wrote on auto repair manuals, billing envelopes, discarded boxes, plasterboard, scrap paper, and wooden boards and planks.

The actions of these brave, caring, and learned adults drew me closer to their creativity, ideas, and imagination. First and foremost, they were my guides, models, and teachers; they invited me to join them and practice in becoming a dreamer, scribe, and poet. Thus, long ago I followed the creative, dancing, and glowing mind.

Imagination enlivens so much that I feel energized as I create, yet stillness is just as nourishing for the creative spirit. Poetry provides a path to create among the children, adolescents, and adults who surround me and keep me going. The poems in these pages are braided from many creative energies, spirits, and stories. Overall, poetry can summon and guide readers inward and to new directions.

"Desde su agujero de arcilla escuchó el eco de las voces que lo llamaban y, como si de grillos se tratara, intentó ubicar a cada hombre dentro de los límites del olvidar. Berreos como jaras calcinadas. Tumbado sobre un costado, su cuerpo en forma de zeta se encajaba en el hoyo sin dejarle apenas espacio para moverse."

—Jesús Carrasco, una selección de *Intemperie: Una novela* (2013)

"From inside his hole in the ground, he heard the echoes calling his name and, as if they were crickets, he tried to pinpoint the precise location of each man within the bounds of the olive grove. The desolate howls of fire-scorched scrub. Lying on one side, he had his knees drawn up to his chest in a Z-shape and with barely enough room to move in the cramped space."

—Jesús Carrasco, *Out in the Open: A Novel*
(excerpt translated by R. Joseph Rodríguez)

I.
Remember and Pronounce

And remembering . . .
Remembering, with twinklings and twinges,
As they lean over the beans in their rented back room that
    is full of beads and receipts and dolls and cloths,
    tobacco crumbs, vases and fringes.

—Gwendolyn Brooks (1917–2000),
from "The Bean Eaters" (1959)

Henrietta Lacks: HeLa
(after reading Skloot)

Ethics
we learn
with your immortal
existence
and care
across cells
living
and breathing
your name.

Rest assured
you are
our fundamental
breath
in times
of biopsies
and mitosis.

You connect
us
all.
Live on.

Movements
your cells create
and remind us
that we
are made
of stars
and you.

In immortality
rest alive

and known
as we bow
alive
with you.

terra nostra

if the land could speak
what would she say
ever wonder

would she ask to be cleansed
bleached away
watered down
cleared of debris
or freed of bloody battles
ever wonder

would she moan for a drink
of rain on her round body
or a taste of some freedom
on her soil

maybe she would holler
loudly or shout thunder
she could be speechless
but not without emotion

maybe she would bubble
into tears and dissolve
from hard earth to loose sand
that would rise
and disappear in the thinness
of the cool air

or would she ask us
to look down her throat
to swallow us?

at Sierra de los Mansos
(after reading Lucille Clifton)

nobody says the names
the given names by native peoples
to rocks once moved so moved
by the people calling this home
now unidentified and indistinct
instead we only hear of purchases
and treasures galore of land
the ranger remembers with glories
claimed yet he does not know
the names we know of the sacred
rocks and hands once touching earth
some bodies sat here and carved
mountains of lineage with rocks
fed fish and manna on these rocks
how waters once flooded the land
shaping rocks and adobe we behold
before us as we ascend into the sky
and rock bed flowers bloom
we know the rocks must know
their own deserted names
and our ancestral names
even if we misremember
or forget to ask what pages
were rewritten without us
without telling what was
and is native and holy here
somebody manifested another
telling by making one history
after the coming of franklin in 1848
erasing some memories and names
we remember and pronounce

Rites for Gregorio Cortez
for Américo Paredes (1915–1999), in memoriam

They still sing of him . . .
—**Américo Paredes**, from *"With His Pistol in His Hand"*:
A Border Ballad and Its Hero (1958)

Chased him through the once barren Texas land.
Tried to shoot him. Many against one.
Those bullets may stop some,
But not him. His hand
Is quick, mightier than the bullet.
He was a man, a vaquero. He was on his own,
Brave, for that is why he is well-known.
Rode his mare through the thicket,
Was a ranger on the range, too,
And practically promenaded the prairie.
Too real of a man—too robust came he
Riding, riding he flew and grew
Into a Mexican folk ballad.
Now again comes he riding, not sad,
But loudly lassoing the plains with the wind.
He is taming the wild land
With his pistol in his hand.

las abuelitas

hand in hand
or arm in arm
warmed by brown bony bones
wrapped under peacock-colored
shawls, they share words
about the past
long-gone
only held by threads
of yesterday
& bleaching black & white
photographs of once full faces
& full figures
now in different forms
that come with wrinkles
of time
& creaky bones
now leaning on canes
but still holding on
& walking
       walking . . .

El día de los muertos

As we dead awaken,
celebrate our birth, dance
with the glaring of the sun
under the moonlit night,
singing songs of México.
Light flames in our name.
Let lyrical laughter
whirl round our bodies
along with sonrisas of children
warming our live bodies
as we sway together in celebration.

Watch us rise from our tombs
to savor the earthy wines of life.

Brother's Propaganda

IED: A simple bomb made and used by unofficial or unauthorized forces.

Origin
1970s: short for improvised explosive device.
—*Oxford English Dictionary* (2019)

Always a game at the beginning.
To groom me. No choices
on the battleground for play.
Indian I am assigned, though
vaquero I'd prefer. He charges,
guns down, then leaves casually.
I surrender boy self and stance.
Hollywood's his 70s primer,
an essential element.
He tastes false victories.
Soon other words name me,
hurled like sharpened machetes,
or shrapnel from IEDs.
I know us no more.
Bad guys from screens
and wars he imitates.
He becomes them,
officiates with authority.
I ask him my name,
to now call me by all
my chosen names,
some christened,
as he wears down
spilling with ideations
after service and war,
in locked solitude,
in the shoe.

Aplausos

Memory is a complicated thing, a relative to truth, but not its twin.
—Barbara Kingsolver

Father unloads the cartridges from the Winchester. One is jammed, but that is unknown. He aims toward the floorboard, but then adjusts his aim toward the lower part of the dining room wall. He pulls the trigger. All is dust. I scream. Siblings huddle by my feet. The bullet scraped my ankle through the living room wall and out the front door. I am on the carpeted floor, bleeding. The drywall dust dances in the light. Mother is not here. She has already left us. The neighbors descend upon the house. It was the TV, Father explains. *Aplausos,* he says. Too much applause from the television set. Father sends them away and then towers above us. Look, it's nothing at all, he pleads for me to say, too. *Nada.* Father walks away. Alone, he sits at the head of the table then covers his face with his hands.

The Yellow Kitchen

at abuelita's, Waelder, Texas, Gonzales County

We ran in there as kids at play
with a ruckus and racket
across creaky floorboards
announcing our house entrance.
Through the snaky hallway,
we reached the kitchen
where abuelita cooked foods
and tended to her cotton linens
and pots and pans and spoons
to serve others and, last, herself.

Every gesture was a communion
with children and adults alike
who came to her for sustenance
and direction when no compass
gave a reading of what was next.
What's next? we'd ask her
in muted tones or hidden speech.

We wanted to know and know
what followed in the schema
of living and life. She knew.
Her yellow kitchen gave us
safety, reprieve, hope.

We look back and see her, now,
through the rearview mirror,
waving her hand blessing
on our journey eastbound.
The car hisses down FM-1296,
to U.S. Highway 90, then I-10,
homeward bound to Houston.

in honor of Helen Nava Rodríguez (August 18, 1920–October 10, 2011)

Recuerdo: Say, "Cheese!"

Much earlier than our arrival to school,
they assemble their equipment
and set up in the temporary buildings
miniature photo studios for us.
We climb into their space for portraits
we later retrieve and remember—years
ago while growing up. Well, no one
then owned a camera in our homes
to capture these moments and events.

These photographers bring smiles
and pull us out of our sleepiness
and mornings to smile before them
and for our families working far
away in the factories or refineries,
ready to bring dollars for a memory.

Look here, honey, we tell our spouse.
*That's when I was in school and grinned
for a quick photo. Yes, that tooth I lost.
Why'd I miss kickball over this? I missed
playing marbles and the races to get in line.*

Our smiles now translate as thank yous
to the eager photographers who rose
much earlier than we for memories
they knew outlast a moment's flash.

To Father

after the ICU
after the velorio
after the rosary
after the mass
after the burial
at the camposanto
you wave adiós
you rise as a traveler
onto the next world now
seeking more tranquility
and refills for your coldest
most favored brews
and aged brandies

The Father's Prayer

Father, who is out there,
holy is your name mostly.
Your kingdom was here.
You did what you could
and provided
mostly at our table.
Tempted you were
all around.
Bills and debts grew.
Adversaries abound.
May your power
and glory
be measured
in time.

Last Will and Testament

The document arrives
via US mail
in a canary envelope
for my signature
all official and certified—
and not like a divorce decree
via a courier of bad news.

One George Washington bill
Father bequeaths
to three
of five children
we know.

FEDERAL RESERVE NOTE

THIS NOTE IS LEGAL TENDER
FOR ALL DEBTS, PUBLIC AND PRIVATE

Of all the bills,
why a George Dubyah?
Why's providence undertaken
as favorable for currency?

A whole dollar
someone
will be mailing
or dropping off soon.

And what if
I'm not home
to receive
the federal reserve note
in my right hand?

Who will hold
Father's tender gesture
until my arrival?

One More to Tell: Una más para contar

—*Tráeme otra, mi'jo.*

—Bring me another one, my son.

The request comes. I am bid. I am called to serve. Here among the boys and girls is the interrupted boy. Look at him closely with one ear at the game, one for father's call. Ears attuned. Employed at eight he is. He serves even if the ball comes for bat, catch, or kick. Hide-and-seek game sends me behind the garage, but I am called mid-count. Ready or not's not here. Pause the game NOW. This is my calling now. Older siblings are saved from duties and flee far from here. I am left, youngest son. A FINE PILSNER BEER from the Frigidaire I fetch. Unopened I handle the can, a cylinder of aluminum might. I plan to deliver. Obedient I can be, but also resistor. I shake my body, can in hand, oh, we shake. Shakable. I walk with the can and hand it over. Here is your drink, I wanna say. Here. He holds it near, and I wait. I want the can opened as I stand behind the screened door. Open it, open it NOW. The foam gushes as a geyser as I grin from afar. *¡Este muchacho fregado!* My freedom to play arrives. I must bat, catch, kick, and, well, serve.

II.
Occupation

Living is no laughing matter:
    you must live with great seriousness
        like a squirrel, for example—
I mean without looking for something beyond and above living,
        I mean living must be your whole occupation.

      —Nazim Hikmet (1902–1963), from "On Living" (1948)

To St. Paul

Among the stones overturned
and recalling my catechism,
forced faith of conviction,
I walk in the open—
unjudged and free.

Ecclesia whispers
and affirmations of faith,
prayers to the sky and sun
a giving of bountiful thanks
by citizens of the day,
by me once for baptism,
later the Lamb and wine,
a sacred oath of allegiance.

I walk on now
far from home
here in Corinth
as Tejano,
Chicano,
Latino,
U.S. citizen,
son of the Américas,
and Corinthian (for a day).

Address me here, St. Paul—
en vivo—
and let your words
speak to love
and remembering
whose life
we are to imitate.

Trinidad: Papá, Dad y el Papa

Oh, madre mía, these three gave our world orders
and told you when to make and serve the hors d'oeuvres.
They fed you what to be, say, do, and follow
until you obeyed them and they filled your hollow.
Mother, tell me the hallelujahs you keep in time.
What is your untold story and prayer and rhyme?
With whom did you cry and share when I was a boy?
I'd ask you about you, but you'd give me a toy
to distract me or read me a story; or say
something equally important for the whole day:
it was time to make dinner before Dad arrived
from the refinery dusty with hands fisted;
or, if lucky, he'd be in the very best mood.
He'd come home to a waiting wife who understood
and two tall daughters and two sons who went unheard.
Only adult voices were heard; nothing else stirred.
I disagreed with the Bible stories you read
when I asked about the willing wives the men had.
I got easily distracted by the unsaid
and wanted to write the other story instead.
Mother, were the sacraments all you were promised?
And what shall we keep and follow from your life lived?
I'd ask this and more if your life had not ended.
So much you left behind, both done and untended.
Oh, madre mía, these three gave our world orders
and told you when to make and serve the hors d'oeuvres.

She's Gone

My mother's gone
to be among the women.

Sisters accompany her
in moments like these.

Father's furies and fists
left her black and blue.

What's she to do quarterless
in the Kroger parking lot?

The children cry and plead.
Father's immune to them.

In fact, he's plotting again
his next moves and torments.

My mother's Lot's mother.
She's not alone in the world.

A long line of mothers sit
beside her and nod meekly.

On bare feet mother carries
souls to safer grounds.

Her work's undone and due.
Watch her return and rise again.

El día de todos los santos vivos
miércoles, 1º de noviembre de 2006

Este día te recuerdo, tía abuela Esmerenciana.
Tus preguntas sobre mis deseos y anhelos
me sorprendían.

Me conocías bien antes de conocerme a mí mismo.
Deseos guardaba.

—¿Cuándo vas a casarte, mi hijo?

      ¿Cuándo, cuándo, cuándo?

—No sé, tía abuela. Un día de estos.

      Un día de estos, un día de estos, un día de estos.

—¿Qué esperas?

      Por qué no me preguntabas:
      "¿A quién esperas?"

Nunca supe cómo responderte.

      "No quiero una esposa que me espose,"
      te hubiera dicho, pero aún no era un poeta.

En el fondo de mi ser, quería un esposo que me esposara.

El día de todas las almas
jueves, 2º de noviembre de 2006

Durante sus últimos días, mi tía abuela me preguntó:

—¿Vestirás santos? ¡Ay, déjate vivir!

Desvisto santos. No santas.
Pensé dentro de mí.
Me quedé mudo.

Mañana, me preguntarán:

—¿Eres casado, jóven?

—No, no soy, les diré.

Why the Moon Is Crescent

The moon was not always crescent shaped.

There once lived Chac Mool who used the full moon to light his path through the night as a lantern.

One day, the moon said she would be moved by no one, not even by the sun, so she stayed put, round in open space.

Then, the sun rose dripping his gold, and the moon was no longer needed. He stopped right in front of the moon.

Next, they shared words and light until the sun decided to take some light away from the moon.

The sun took more than half the moon's light, leaving her oddly shaped.

The moon grew pale and crossed the sky to the other side of the world.

She, the moon, refused to be moved by the sun. He, the sun, slowly took her energy, melting her heart.

The day is his, and the night is hers.

So, this is how it happened. In fact, this is why there are eclipses and white nights.

Chac Mool passed this story and many others through his people.

This is just one of the stories I was told and that I have put down on paper.

Endangered Species

> I am a word
> in a foreign language.
> —**Margaret Atwood**, from "Disembarking at Quebec" (1970)

When you speak of Aztlán,
my soul rises and my bones ache.
You say Aztlán was and is this and that to me
and I own no words to speak of Aztlán,
a land unknown to me.
The only Aztlán I have ever known
is America. I have a Spanish surname
that you say traces
to indigenous peoples
who own no terrain in their lands.
You speak with thick and slippery syllables
and ancient foreign accents that slide,
slithering from your articulate mouth.
Náhuatl you say is a part of your brown bones
and soverign soul.
Tenochtitlán and Chichén Itzá you mention
and I, carnal,
do not know of what you speak;
I am a foreigner.
You speak about los olmecas, zapotecas, toltecas,
chichimecas, mayas, and aztecas
whose civilizations you say flourished
before the Spaniards and other tyrants
came to the New World.
You say we are all peninsulares, criollos, or mestizos.
There is no carnalismo.
Carnal, unlike you, I was born and bred north of the Río Grande.
You name Cristóbal Colón, Hernán Cortés, Francisco Vásquez de Coronado,
Álvar Núñez Cabeza de Vaca, Bartolomé de las Casas, Sor Juana Inés de la Cruz

Miguel Hidalgo, José María Morelos, Antonio López de Santa Ana,
and Agustín de Iturbide as if they are at the tip
of your tongue and I, carnal,
I with my American entangled tongue and mashed mind,
am endangered in this strange land.

Frozen

I walk the aisles
looking for a chilled dessert.
Escalofríos braille my skin
and numb my ears, fingers.
I jet down the aisle
to a cooler that announces
with signage above me
"Frozen Hispanic"
to shoppers with carts to fill.

Would a Disney movie
be stored in one
of these coolers?
Nope. A fantasy.
Who's frozen now
in my walk? I find Amy's
Cheese Enchilada. ¡Olé!
Made with organic tortillas
and gluten-free
for a non-glutton.
¡Bravo!

Should I keep
walking down
a few more aisles
and find a Disney
Frozen DVD
and freeze it here
like a joker
with a vandal mind?
Winter into eternity?

Let me Tweet
about this now

like a mobile
blue bird @target.
Let me unfreeze
my mind now
and attempt
a change of language
via social media action.
Here I will fly.

Homeland Insecurity

> "US builds migrant tent city in Texas as Trump likens influx to 'Disneyland'"
> —headline from *The Guardian*, April 29, 2019

Dear Policymakers, Políticos, and Congress in Regress:

Free the children, mothers, and fathers
from your grip and contracts.

The USA still occupies and extorts their lands.

Bring our children, mothers, and fathers home.
This is our summons now.

We await your promise
of freedom in compromised lands.

Sincerely,
We the People
(across the USA and abroad)

Galut
at Tornillo

A chorus of citizens
quilts the children
under tents
in the cold.

The children wait
in cages
for mothers
and fathers moving
across continental plates.

Here arms outstretch,
far from Galilee
in the Chihuahuan Desert
winter and creosote.

The chorus rises—flor
y canto—for the children
coming home
at last
to be clothed
in familiar warmth
and love.

Anthem

Oh, America, can you see and notice us, standing before you?
On your lands and shores we arrive: tossed into detention
for a place at your table and in your pages of history.
Who's a pioneer or settler now? We migrate to your door
for inalienable rights and truths so self-evident.
Stories you cover and hide like our face and labor.
See us now and be the liberty that enlightens the world.

In the News
(or WTF?! / No Sh##, Sherlock!)

'Men explain things to me.'

With bags of cash, CIA seeks influence in Afghanistan

Afghan leader confirms cash deliveries by CIA

CIA 'buys influence with bags of cash' left at office of Afghan President Hamid Karzai

Contractors reap $138bn from Iraq war

20 companies profiting the most from war

The US Department of Justice just shut down a huge asset forfeiture program by law
    enforcement

Confederate statues removed across southern US states

Golden age superheroes were shaped by the rise of fascism

College can be hard on your mental health. Here's are 7 ways to cope.

Changing more than pronouns: A non-binary teen fights education laws

'I want to go out as someone who spoke the truth.'

'Sorry, but I am too busy to talk to you right now.'

Seven baby monkeys died from poisoning at US research center

Afghan Defense Ministry: US leaflet drop broke agreement

Led not into temptation: Pope Francis approves changes to Lord's Prayer

Trump appears in front of doctored seal with Russian and golf imagery

Before Flint, before East Chicago, there was Smeltertown

Offers pour in to cover PA students' meal debt, but school officials not interested.

Immigrant kids fill this town's schools. Their bus driver is leading the backlash.

My 24 years without eating (nearly) vegetables

Women are being told lies about their bodies

Bruce Lee's daughter hits out at father's portrayal in Tarantino film

In the 21st century, we are all migrants

US writers recall their migrant journeys in protest at asylum seekers' treatment

'We met in Queens, as kids. Decades later, we reunited, as authors.'

'I read Dostoevsky and Solzhenitsyn when I was 10.'

Why we should listen to teenagers speak about climate crisis

Why it's time to stop worrying about the decline of the English language

Teacher education needs to acknowledge 'Whiteness.'

The backlash to MTV/s 'White People' shows why it needed to be made

The FBI could fight the far-right if they wanted to—but they don't.

A new history tears down the myth of the Texas Rangers.

Pink seesaws reach across the divide at US–México border

Texas has a long history of anti-Mexican racism. My family lived it.

The idea that Latinx people constitute an 'invasion' in the US is nothing new.

To understand the El Paso massacre, look to the long legacy of anti-Mexican violence at the border.

A mouse fell from the ceiling at the White House.

Make healthy eating easy thanks to this technique used by the US Army.

'Forgotten by society': How Chinese migrants built the Transcontinental Railroad

Lawmakers respond to 'vile,' secret Facebook group created by US Border Patrol agents.

'I almost got killed': The Hmong refugees who call the US home

An expert on concentration camps says that's exactly what the US is running at the border.

Trump administration argues detained migrant children don't need toothbrushes, soap.

From Libya to Texas, tragedies illustrate plight of migrants.

A father and daughter who drowned at the border put attention on immigration.

This photo is about bodies—migrant bodies. Don't look away.

Migrant child drawings depict scenes of detention.

At detention camps and shelters, art helps migrant youths find their voices.

'I don't care' if migrants are held for '400 days.'

'Put politics aside, consider the plight of migrant children.'

US builds migrant tent city in Texas as Trump likens influx to 'Disneyland.'

One of the oldest known human settlements Hasankeyf is about to be swallowed whole.

Calls for Kavanaugh's impeachment come amid new misconduct allegations.

The US Secretary of Education Betsy DeVos reverses course on Special Olympics cuts after Trump orders funding.

DeVos puts protecting for-profit schools ahead of students.

Teacher's union head calls DeVos handling of student loan forgiveness program 'a travesty.'

Working nights to pack your California Strawberries, working days to graduate from school

Caliban never belonged to Shakespeare.

Ancestral home of modern humans is in Botswana, study finds.

Americans aren't using their homes as piggy banks anymore.

Hundreds of Facebook employees to CEO Mark Zuckerberg: "Free speech and paid speech are not the same thing."

The seven-year auto loan: America's middle class can't afford their cars.

'I don't regret enforcing the law': US Department of Homeland Security Secretary Kirstjen Nielsen defends family separation at summit.

Every child can become a lover of books.

Ditch the grammar and teach children storytelling instead.

Moving stories: Inside the book buses changing children's lives.

ACLU says 1,500 more migrant children were taken from parents by the Trump administration.

Florida county refuses to pay for The New York Times in public libraries: 'It's fake news.'

'A lot of guys think every woman wants to sleep with them.'

The end of generations of exploitation by the NCAA is finally in sight.

'A climate denier-in-chief sits in The White House today. But not for long.'

'By shirking its responsibility to filter out lies, Facebook is a threat to civic society.'

Facebook rebrands as FACEBOOK: Can capital letters save a toxic brand?

Far-right leader and Washington officers face civil rights lawsuit over violent incident.

Impeachment inquiry transcripts reveal shock and concern over Trump plot.

'We finished every bottle!' Berlin's cultural legends on the night the Wall came down.

Conquistadors tumble as indigenous Chileans tear down statues.

The Anti-Mask League: lockdown protests draw parallels to 1918 pandemic

Can a face mask protect me from coronavirus? Covid-19 myths busted

As hot spots shift, Covid-19 pandemic enters a new phase.

George Floyd killing: police officer charged with third-degree murder and manslaughter

U.S. Foreign Policy
for Tom Raworth

This poem has been removed for a new occupation.

A Teacher Dreams with His Students

In the beginning there is light
and two wide-eyed figures standing
near the foot of your bed,
and the sound of their voices is love.
          —Matt de la Peña, from *Love* (2018)

Tue., 5th September 2017

Dear Students and Teachers,
I open my journal to write about my teaching day.
My students tell me their summons will come.
Their crime is to fulfill their dream of learning
in this country they and others now call home.

And what do I tell them tomorrow when I write
on the whiteboard an essential question for the day?
Who's essential? Who survives? Who cares?
And who declares which Dreamers can stay?

Cautiously you tell me your mornings begin.
Each early dawn brings many fears and plans.
Each day comes with a horizon and sundown.
Hope you carry high in your hearts and hands.

Another semester will come, and this classroom
is our safe and keeping place. Come, stay here.
Your dreams and journeys are yours and ours.
As your teacher I will be the hull and steer.

The Friendly Store: L'arte di lavorare
April 18, 1984

This is where I really want to work for good,
I tell myself at ten. *Quiero trabajar por mí mismo.*
Tengo que hacerlo. A firm push on the heavy,
swollen wooden door brings a friendly greeting
from the lady behind the counter in glasses
and a hair bun and who smiles and greets Father,
"Well, hello, Mr. Pete! How are you today?"
"O, just fine. Thank you. Good to see you."
There's a smile and wave for the children here.
Father gathers groceries we need and a few vices
of his own. Language comes alive here, everywhere!
So many words appear and blink and get jumbled
in my head, and then words crisscross and somersault
and do English backflips here: Chiquita bananas,
La Predilecta tortillas, gummy bears, Dr Pepper and
Coke and Pepsi and Tab sodas, Huggies diapers,
homemade Italian sausage, po' boy sandwiches,
Poinsettia milk, Carnation milk, PET evaporated milk,
brown eggs, Gerber jarred baby food, Ex-Lax, cottage
cheese, Hanes t-shirts, filtered cigarettes, Pepto-Bismol,
Fritos, Funyuns, Vicks VapoRub, Tres Flores Brilliantine,
Alka-Seltzer, Tylenol, mineral water, Rolaids, Tums,
Payday and Snickers bars, Hubba Bubba Bubble Gum,
peanut butter bars, Chips Ahoy! cookies, Rainbo bread,
Blue Bell ice cream, Push-Up pops, Drumstick cones,
freshly cut meats, iceberg lettuce, white onions, garlic.
Carrabba's Friendly Grocery, since 1955, serves us here.
At the counter, the school photos of neighborhood girls
and boys adorn the tier-rack of chewing gum for all to see
at time to pay. A card of St. Jude Thaddaeus is on display
with bright eyes aglow, all-seeing, a halo adorns his head.

So much light here and the warm people, yes, who know
each other and what they seek and want for their families.
Words and wants brand my head into memory as Father
and I walk the aisles of our neighborhood grocery store.
The butcher shop lists prices by the lbs. and sliced meats
from the delicatessen. Rodríguez sausage is sold here.
Our name on the label stands out, so proudly. The man
who makes the Italian sausage and cuts all the meats
must be off today. His laughter and radio are missed.
Only the lady in the bun is here with her customers.
Rosie! they say in song when they see her. Everything
is here that we want and need. *Where else is there to go?*
By now, Father grabs a pack of La Ranchera Corn Tortillas.
I think about the job I want as Father presses me to get
courage if I want to work here, to speak up, to stand up.
We reach the eye-level counter for my moment to speak.
—*Dile, mi'jo, dile.* "Tell her what you're thinking,
son." At ten? I am thinking of English words now to say
that are coming in stages. Well, then, I speak in words
new to me that make me stammer, but sound like I know
what I want. "Ma'am, I want to work here. Can I?"
"Well, baby, let me think." "Please, please!" I throw in.
"I can do just about anything." I am out of ideas really.
"Well, come back next Wednesday after school.
Your dad can drop you off for a couple of hours."
"Thank you, ma'am." I want to do a dance, but instead
run to the truck to tell my eldest sister who also works.
I am going to learn what work is, what happens here.

Houston, Texas

to janet adeleye

touch the lit
keypad and dial
the 800 number
and voilà
janet appears
like a genie
at microsoft
covering
the whole world
and iss
high above
in orbit
but here is janet
in voice

far from texas
we speak
to get
my surface laptop
working again
as she shows
tech magic
with warm cues
and utmost respect
toward me
sharing my keyboard
and screen
she troubleshoots
with results

where are you now, janet?
i ask
west africa
she answers politely

and i wonder
how in the world
i got to meet janet
how can this be
the luck we share
to speak
and wait
as the machine does
its thing
for a new installation
and updates
and starts
working again

but the best part
is janet
who i meet
and whose laugh
is genuine
and gentle
and real
and i am grateful
to janet to pen
this poem
and send to her
one day soon
via email
to the cradle
of our civilizations
and universe
that began
with a tone
and dial

can you believe
what happens
on this
small earth
we call home?

III.
Interrogation

[S]igo haciendo preguntas que quedan sin respuesta. Y creo que
moriré con un punto de interrogación impreso bajo los párpados.

—**Elena Poniatowska (1991)**

I keep asking questions that have no answers. I think I will die
with a question mark engraved on my eyelids.

—**Elena Poniatowska** *(translation by R. Joseph Rodríguez)*

Rivers of Languages

Rivers of languages

        los ríos de idiomas

flow here

       past deltas and borders and boundaries

                 into towns and cities

          rise in homes and libraries and schools,

              voices rising like poetry and bread.

Languages remind us where we begin.

Everyjuan/x

arises
before coffee drips
everywhere
faces grace hell
idle justice
knows limits
memorizes
notices
opportunities
permanent
qualification
restores
sanity
thinks
underdog
vows
winning
xenagogue
yearns
zapateo

In Heaven
after Dickinson's poem #1096,
"These Strangers in a foreign World"

In heaven
        refugee I'll be
                a reminder
of my lineage
        and more families
                before me
tongues forsaken
        names reversed
                books torn
to belong briefly
        as accepted citizens
                in communities
or as temporary residents
        in shifting eyes
                always watchful
yet pilgrim am I
        forever traveler
                and walking forward:
                        homeward bound.

Assessment and Evaluation
after seeing Sir John Everett Millais's painting
Bubbles: A Child's World (1886)

At the kitchen table,
Benjamin places
a yellow Post-it note
and pencil in my hands.

As if by genius instinct,
his quick hand is followed
by a pointed gesture for me
to begin the assignment.

"Joey, Joey!" he calls.
"Write me some questions, okay?
Write me some questions!"

His voice invites me
to work beside him
as his unstoppable
curiosity and energy
bubble up.

Ben's six.
"What kinds of questions do you want?"
He grimaces, and his brown eyes extra blink.

"The kinds with bubbles to pick the right
answer. Hmm, like this, look!"

He takes a pencil in hand,
shapes and curves letters to words.
Soon symbols appear in pairs
with chords and harp strings

to make sentences bellowing
with meaning and commands.

Ben creates a question.
One bubble here with words, then another.
The bubbles appear clear, precise.
Round. Circles. Ready to be filled in,
to torment with choices. A through D.

Bubbles balloon before us as he blots them.
Multiple masteries appear before our eyes.
The question stem gets written with options.
All adds up: three distractors and, yes,
of course, the correct one, the key.

Ben commands, "Now you, okay? Now you,
Joey!"

His watermelon grin invites me
to write precisely and for results.
He hovers over my shoulder. I struggle.
Bubbles must soon surface for blotting.

"What about the other kinds of questions?"
I ask.

"Which ones?" Ben wants to know.

"I want to write some without bubbles, like,
'Tell me a story about an elf.'
Or 'How do you know if a dinosaur's really a dinosaur?'"

"Okay, write them," Ben says.
I draft a list:
1. Describe what Fuzzy and Lucy like to read.
2. Why do Fuzzy and Lucy ride in a truck?
3. Tell me about Elfie.
4. How many dinosaur teeth do you have?

On a few sticky notes, Ben writes:

1. Lucy likes to read *Charlet Wed*. Fuzzy
   likes to read trucks.
2. Lucy and Fuzzy love to ride in a truck
   because they like to read in it.
3. Once upon a time there was an elf named
   Elfie. And he lives in the north Pole.
   He went to a boy named Ben. Elfie is nice
   and kind.
4. I have one.

"It's time to eat, Ben," his mother calls and waits.

Ben leaves our writing table,
grabs the bubbles solution.
Off he goes, running inside
with a wand in hand.

Self in 1985

(variation on a theme by Anne Sexton, 1928–1974)

What is real?
I am a boy; I stand
with eyes that are brown and shining without heavy hurt or fall
upon some other timid yet haunting boys,
eyes that close, open, spin, and close.
Am I appropriately a boy? Kmart transfixed?
I have hair, raven black,
thin legs, lanky arms
and some resale clothes.

I study in a school
with twenty-six desks
two chalkboards, two windows,
three closed closets and one big door.
Many of you have come to this place.
There is a big desk,
(for the lead teacher)
a tiled floor,
windows that open to the playground and temporary buildings,
and rows of shotgun houses and crisscrossing streets.

Someone taunts me,
plants an open blow on my head,
What is it Antonio said afterward?
Someone adult pretends not to see nor feel with me—
I am alone among them—
or cast aside in another space.
They ignore me!
Their coy kindness? Their kindness is not real!
They keep me silent to their taunts
and their hurt.

What is real
to this fifth-grade boy
who should play, who should fit in,
should be boy-like in a wholesome school,
and have no evidence of other or pain?
But I would cry, too,
bound into existence and walls that
were once my uncles and aunts
if I could know then
and if I had the heart.

Visiting the Rijksmuseum
for Ms. Lennie Otuemhobe, high-school art teacher extraordinaire

All the art
from school
textbooks
comes alive
before the canvas
of my eyes
gazing
across rooms.

I surrender
to Rembrandt's
The Night Watch
without turning
a page.
Instead, I stand
here
noticing
the chiaroscuro.
What contrasts to my eyes!

I become
lost on purpose
with rooms
newly rearranged.

Rooms
with canvases
bloom and open
to more art
that began
with a noble
welcome
from Christophle
le More.

Eres

Quiero amarte. Atarte. Amarrarte.
—**Sandra Cisneros**, from "You Bring Out the Mexican in Me" (1994)

Eres dulce y húmedo.
Así te recuerdo.

Te he memorizado
como un papalote en el horizonte,
como un globo rojo flotando en el aire
hasta que llega a su destino
en los brazos del que lo espera.

El aire lleva tu nombre.

Eres y sigues siendo.

Te persigo

No sé cuál de los dos escribe esta página.
—**Jorge Luis Borges (1899–1986)**, una selección de "Borges y yo" (1960)

Te persigo en mis sueños.
Quiero sentirte bajo mis alas.

Un día de estos te alcanzaré.
Un día de estos, un día de estos . . .

Heart Drum

Disfruta, come y bebe, que la vida es breve.

Lead me to your well of rum
to be merry and free:
before your gaze,
hearing your heart drum.

You are my ardent liquor:
my intoxicant ingredient,
my excess, my spirit,
my mezcal.

And today is to be lived,
arm in arm,
or hand in hand—
unafraid, and
unrestrained.

I yearn for your sugary molasses.
Come, my heart-runner,
let's raise our glasses
and drink and be merry,
full of gaiety.

Para todo mal, mezcal, y para todo bien también.

Autobiografía literaria

"¡YO PERDURARÉ!"
from *I Am Joaquín: An Epic Poem* (1967)

"I SHALL ENDURE!"
selección de *Yo soy Joaquin: Un poema épico* (1967)
—**Rodolfo "Corky" Gonzales (1928–2005)**

Listen, Mom and Dad.
Escúchenme, Mami y Papi.

I am who I am: a gay man.
Soy gay y seguiré siéndolo.

I know and feel who I am.
Sé y siento quién soy.

This I know well.
Fíjense bien.

This whole life awaited me.
Esta vida entera me esperaba.

Once I hid behind the folds of my arms.
Antes me escondía cruzando los brazos.

I had to come out to myself.
Tenía que salir del armario de mi mismo.

Today I stand facing the sun.
Hoy frente al sol les confieso.

Set apart like a warrior I march onward.
Camino adelante como un guerrero.

Priests and popes chastise my world.
Los sacerdotes y papas castigan mi mundo.

I surrender Vatican cities of secrets and solid gold.
 Renuncio a ciudades vaticanas repletas de secretos y oro.

Sorrow hurts in the past.
 La lástima lastima en el pasado.

Mint heals me through morning.
 La hierbabuena me sana por la mañana.

This is the life I am meant to live.
 Ésta es la vida que debo vivir.

Who would have imagined this?
 ¿Quién se lo hubiera imaginado?

I couldn't imagine myself then to now. Imagine!
 No me imaginaba en ese entonces hasta hoy. ¡Imagínense!

I am Alive, Alive, Alive!
 ¡Viví, vivo y viviré!

I give you my Word.
 Les doy mi Palabra.

The Spanish Teacher
(variation on a theme by Billy Collins)

Trying to protect his students' inocencia
he tells them if they conjugate verbs correctly
they can become learned across the Américas
and that Pablo Picasso spoke Castilian Spanish
while painting *Guernica* about a famous restaurant.

And that Spanish explorers spent lots of time
on tours of war for gold and to rename indigenous
lands in honor of their wives who stayed home,
like Queen Isabella, spinning a teary shroud,
counting all the days and nights to a listening Dios.

The Spanish expelled no one in 1492, rather they
pushed to sail three ships with honorable names
to feed the world warm gazpacho and tapas for all.
Some students interrupt and ask, "Well, then,
how come España just this year attempted to atone
for 500-hundred-plus-year-old sins? The Jews, Moors?"
"And what about the Basque, then, your excellency?"

The most bullying, hard-headed students clamored
to mute all the inquisitors before them and, as if
by remote control, they acquiesced, since expulsion
loomed until voices quivered and none questioned.

The teacher gathered his devices and placed them
in his murse and—with a wily cybersmile of sorts—
walked gingerly down the hall, exiting the building
into the just-swept streets, wondering if his students
would one day visit España and savor the Rioja wines.

In Academia

1

"I've never met an assistant to a professor.
What's that like?"

2

"It's not enough to work hard to get tenure here.
Remember that. Work smart. And watch your back."

3

"Here, the gold medal is for research, silver for teaching;
bronze, copper, or less are reserved for service."

4

"Easy, wasn't it, for you to land this job?"

5

"Is your research in the hard sciences?
That's what really counts here."

6

"Well, soft sciences are just that.
Who wants soft anything *really*?"

7

"My Ivy League education sets me apart.
Many don't get one, and that's a shame."

8

"The administrative assistant is powerful
with keys and a keyboard that make everything happen."

9

"Test loyalties here, because they shift
into all forms and shapes. Be alert like a watchman."

10
"Some of our colleagues would perish in the real world.
Hungry or starved they'd be. I wish them the best. I *really* do."

11
"The years go by quick, so publish a lot soon.
Clock ticks. *Hear that?*"

12
"Teaching's for the birds.
Man, that's why I just write grants
and fill the admin's coffers. All's well for me."

13
"If the president is all about student success,
can we add student learning, understanding, and knowledge, too?"

14
"Student affairs may want to consider academics, don't you think?
It's not all university parties or standing committee meetings."

15
"Students used to be able to explore before choosing a major.
Now they get penalized if they don't graduate fast enough."

16
"The third-year review matters the most.
Be sure to fill it up with details and results."

17
"Academia is not about an endless amount of meetings.
Though I admit it looks that way sometimes.
Remember to contribute to the sum of knowledge and community."

18
"Every day can be like a sabbatical in academia."

19
"Write the books and articles fast. Time flies."

20

"What did you say your research is in?
I wasn't quite listening earlier."

To Mrs. Anne Bradstreet

Yes, your house burned down
and, yes, we love our spouses, too.
Tell me more than that please. Will you?
Tell me about the giving people
whose houses also burned, and theirs
weren't teepees as history books say.
Tell me about the coming centuries
foretold with crosses ablaze across scores
of grid system lands, lawns, and porches
in frontiers called rural areas
with some urban and suburban
neighborhoods people call home.
Mention the loaves of bread broken
on supper tables then upturned
for life, liberty, and property.
The poets will bring these stories
once hidden from many people
between poetry lines and safely-
rhymed couplets and stanzas
into the books we call America,
a land of fears and armed bravery.

Captives in White Bone

Colorblind the world comes
as you only see humans
you tell me until—ope!

A rainbow appears
the meteorologist forgot
to announce in the report.

The local school district map's
redrawn for a new tax base
and shift happens suddenly.

And they're here!
The neighbors of color
are not new renters.

Introduce yourself then.
They're the newest homeowners
and also earners and savers.

Life, liberty, and property.
That's in some constitution
or real estate documentation.

Take a look more closely.
Notice the fine print font.
Loans galore America keeps.

Who's captive in a house?
The breadwinner, saver, earner?
Mortgage in French is scary.

A pledge one makes as buyer
as a lien hovers above like a drone.
Color appears encoded and to decode.

Arrangements

"Time to degay the house!" my partner declares.

Must we become someone else? It's as if the infantry is stomping its way, en route, for our boarding boxcars and flatbed trucks.

We can become no one's memory or history in an instant.

It seems so nauseous to concentrate on another season in time and rearrange ourselves and home for the coming—invited and unannounced—guests for the holidays.

We shall be arranged flowers—potted, poised, precise.

Every allowable object shall be in its place, so it sleeps well and looks, well, good on display in high style.

No one's deranged for this composition.

Photos of perfect and enduring matched couples—men-at-arms, women hand-in-hand—shall be removed.

Everything prearranged—arranged, rearranged—like a union.

Oh, to be in love is to be rearranged!

Christmastime it is. The mistletoe is not for our kind to command our lover, Knock me a kiss; lead me to bliss. *Bésame, bésame mucho, papito, bajo este muérdago.*

No kisses in the house, but kisses to keep within until the coast is clear.

What whirls we know not and much less what lurks around the corner, in cloaked legislative sessions.

Everything must be examined and reexamined for possible removal and hidden away for the time being until it is safe to be and assume who we are, our normality. Only the essentials can stay; nothing else.

But our infinite desires intoxicate our being!

Chaos reigns before we perform the glamour of living it easy for our familiar guests. Oh, family! Quick, quick, the merry and gay magazine subscriptions must be removed and any hint of will, grace, and glee must flee from the public eye.

Ooops!—except a forgotten, favorite issue.

—¿Qué es esto? she asks. ("Heavens! What is this?" she would say in horror, in another language, in other words.)

We failed to notice that not everything can be stored away—behind curtains, zipped shut, boxed away in closets and other rooms.

We face the difficult; we run out of space.

So, we open the grand door of the finite temple we house.

Why not be our full selves, embrace ourselves, celebrate ourselves?

We agree, the rearrangements come to an end this Christmastime.

We ride into a new year with a resolution to be ourselves. So, it shall be done.

And let it begin with me.

Keeps
for S.

La imaginación es la loca de la casa.
—**Santa Teresa de Ávila (1515–1582)**

A man to keep and keep keeping
you are. Not beneath the bed to hide
from guest or guide, but on the bed to sleep
and hold and soothe.
And to tangle in the humid sheets
until God's kingdom comes,
until morning.

And neither fox nor horror
distress our sleep,
our bodies in each.

We're like mangoes,
side by side, and aglow in still life.
Our skin ripe and sticky with goo,
a sweet meat for feasting.
Ah, yes, you're for keeps
and sweet devouring.

Tostones
for Seany

Fall from the sky,
tumble and land
in handfuls
on the tin roof.

Like an audience
applause,
the plantains
sing in the hot oil.

Heaven's here
as tostones,
godly gold,
fill our mouths.

Can I, may I
have a second helping?

IV.
Offerings

incense of sun on prairie

to the sky

Breathe the

Offer peace

—**Heid E. Erdrich**, from "Peace Path" (2016)

at the waelder community cemetery

camposanto
holy land
holy site

here is the side
for the burial
of mexicans
true mexicans
if there are such

the sum of many families
lie here
in gonzales county
in tejas

county said
we lie here
nowhere else
this land
is your land
for burials

some unchosen
no matter what
the books say
or extoll
or exhalt
on sábado

there is a line
a demarcation
for the unchosen
not chosen

by abrahán
perhaps maybe

no resting place
on the other side
of the fence
with germans
who once labored
with us and favored
bilingual education

we choose you though
you are chosen
by descendants
and historians
and genealogists

family you shall always be
we remember you
we honor you
despite the fence
with sharpened barbwire
that slits at our skin

you once lay
in rest
and then rose
as scripted

despite human
laws to separate
here is a dugout
facing east
in the land
a plot of land
six feet under
the sun
a star
rises with you too

rest in peace
always

que en paz descansen
siempre

rest in power
forever

que en poder descansen
por siempre

resquiescat in pace

In Memoriam

1980s–today
Am
I
Dying
Solo?

En memoria

de 1980 a la fecha
 Soledad
 Ingrata
¿Debo
 Aguantar?

At the Market

for Vincent Maurice Woodard & in memoriam
(April 21ˢᵗ, 1971–February 4ᵗʰ, 2008)

The produce boy in the green apron winks
as I study the fruits, nuts, and vegetables
he has displayed before my gaze.
I press my fingers on avocado,
mango, and papaya I admire
and hold my grip against flesh.
(Ah, forget the fruit and fall
far from this time and place!)

Today, I am reading produce in braille.
It's not often I am in deep study
beyond pages of tired books
and lined paper calling my name.
I am entranced by my own senses.

I walk on, breathing the hot
and humid tropic and secretly
cling to this harvest on display.
The senses, now mesmerized,
transfix my gaze and cantata.

I see you from the corner of my eye
as I reach for mango and papaya.
Round, ripe, and ready is how I
remember and devour mango
and papaya at times like these.
The succulence streams down
my grinning chin. I know not to bite
but to suck and savor the orange meat,
the yellow meat of still life.

And in pearly union, the onions sit
as pungent bulbs, ready.
If I take knife to their flesh,
my eyes drown, overflow.
Stands like these apprise
a one-man shoppper like me
into oniomania.

Vincent, you are at the tip of my tongue.
I say your name in my daily mantra
as I lean against the produce counter
and think of you and our spring nights:
how we peeled our languid love.

into the fields
Mendota, California

they rise at 4:15 AM
        and out the door they go
                                within minutes
        children, adolescents, parents, grandparents, elders . . .

hurried along
clothed to keep
cool and strong
to moving machinery
and handheld tools
and into the fields
to rows
upon rows
of stooping
and picking
and gathering
all cramped
in the dark
until sunrise
greets them anew

somebody does
honorable work
we must see
we notice
and not look away
as the ground swells
seedlings born

here
right here
look

yes look again
at the hands
knees scorched like earth
arms reaching always
carrying beyond body weight
picking for gathering tables
and changing diets

notice the gatherers
and harvesters
rising early
to sounds of earth
and laborious affairs
awakening the land

hands across hands
bodies next to bodies
alone and along
the seams of earth
and sun beatings
and breathing
and coughing
they bear
all the days
and nights
all the days
and nights

another day
begins again
when the children
and adolescents
rise from the fields
upright and unstoppable
walking toward
school buses

waves of brief goodbyes
begin for another day

and into classrooms
that welcome them
greet them at 8:05 am

the students carry
hidden away
in their backpacks
the bruised and discarded
fruits and vegetables
they then place
on desks
and in the cubicles
for teachers and staff

they know and know
soil and seeds and growth
across the grid systems
with apples and almonds
and the sweetest melons
now in the hands
of those they trust
to learn
and understand more

will you
tell me
who rises
and what grows
despite the aches
and remembers to reach?

if walt whitman

happened to round
the corner
or just sit
on my front porch
to celebrate the songs
of himself
and the multitudes
among us
would it be
a good idea
to call the cops
to round him up
and carry him off
for panhandling
and soliciting
his poems
as he does so boldly
hugging the world
we call *home*?

yes, he carries
some bags
with papers
pencils
holes
oranges
nuts
like a breadgiver.

well, who knows
what i'd do
if he tries
to move on in

and set-up shop
with a loan
from the small
business people's
administration
and open a poetry pantry.

oooooo, right now
the next-door neighbor's got
one of those handheld cameras
on us
with live feed
as she dials 9-1-1
all techy crazed.

oh, boy, really?!
she's made it
her doggone business
to broadcast us.
so i best just sit
and chill here
beside walt
as we get
fully broadcasted,
sin permiso,
mind you,
to the whole wide world
that's always awake
and stirring the pot
all hidden with aliases
behind glowing screens.

just to be clear, officer,
drop that weapon
you're holding:
fellow travelers, are we
who are bound
on our merry way
like troubadours

with flower and song
on a pilgrimage
across many towns?

a Ché

tus manos
las buscamos
y nuestra lucha
sigue
tomados de la mano

a Breiner David Cucuñame
y a los nasa (páez)

caminas
el valle
de cauca
acompañado

sonríes
nos saludas
y haces camino
en estas tierras

das la vuelta
y nos miras
con ojos
penetrantes

eres valiente
por la tierra madre
y como hijo
de los nasa
y de las américas

te acompañamos
en la caminata
para siempre

This Poem Is an Offering to You
(variation on a theme by Jimmy Santiago Baca)

Here is a poem for your reading and keeping,
since I have nothing more to offer you.
Hold this poem and do not release
this poem to the beckoning wind and sky
or water waving for this poem out to sea,
            Te amo. Te adoro.

And I am offering this broccoli floret to you, too,
since, yes, I have run out of vegetables to grow.
Eat it as if it were your last serving from earth
when the staples are gone and foods are scarce
like in recession days of long lines and faces
of despair when the earth no longer gives,
            Te amo. Te adoro.

What can I offer you now but my open arms?
Here they are, my arms outstretched,
reaching outward as if on a cross for you
to walk towards like a child running past
others to the arms of love, warm love,
            Te amo. Te adoro.

There is nothing more to offer you,
and what else is there really to give
in your purpose-driven life
but love held and remembered?
When the devices we use stop cold,
and my arms outstretched for you
will give you warmth and hope and care,
remember:
            Te amo. Te adoro.

ananda balasana

pose
as the happiest
baby-child
of all time

carefree
worriless
so good
a trip in time
playful
lila

remember
the stretch
your joys
then and now
graceful
at ease

adulting yourself
relaxation
calmness
svadisthana
chakra

reach
remember
to reach
awaken
within

A mi amígdala

me acompañas
como amiga
mi almendra proteína
esencial para que sienta
eres mi socio y agente
en mi despertar
me alzas tras mis temores
y gozamos juntos
estarás siempre conmigo
me emociono contigo

to my amygdala

you join me
as mi amiga
almond-like protein
essential for my feelings
you are my associate and agent
for my awakening
with you i rise past my fears
and we are in pleasure together
you shall always be beside me
me emociono contigo

a man

a man enters the Colorado River
        at dusk in the city's edge
looks back
        to nothing in particular
imagines seeing García Márquez's
        handsomest drowned man
beckoning and he keeps walking
        deep into the riverbed
the Austin news reports
        cover his story for a day
viewers and contemplants pause
        and bless his heart

a man wakes at home
        at dawn before alarms and sirens
reaches to awaken
        a child for school
remembers that Sexton's poem
        on wanting and a special language
left him months ago
        he is renewed again
as he finds Sánchez's poem
        on six months after contemplating
storms of life thrust him
        forward again as he
abandons trespasses for generosity
        and mornings bless him

mouths agape
for Jay Dee

your poems rise
from the mojave
dust spins
and bodies rise
arms outstretch
as wind howls
through the desert

we greet with affection
our mouths agape
you feed us
ripened prickly pear

hungry souls are we
long-lost from home
renamed by our own
and forgotten
as unforgiven sons
and daughters
for calling paths
that beckon
and we claim
without looking back

our eyes fill
drown us
and ironed
handkerchief
you offer us
as we gently dab
our brown eyes

love's visible
as mesquite smoke
rising and moving
opening our eyes

we write poems
beside you
our bodies aglow
for the next coming
and calling out
of beloved kin:
our many brothers
and sisters
begin the journey
unforbidden
we bid them

this is our stretch
for our healing heart
becoming whole
love's among us
our breaths one

Los amantes
(from a painting by Pablo Picasso, 1881–1973)

> To be in love
> Is to touch things with a lighter hand.
> —Gwendolyn Brooks (1917–2000), from "To Be in Love" (1963)

The aria of the wind
sends javelins of Cupid
to these two young hearts.

A bond is
within their locked arms.
They look and swim into their eyes.

To warm their blood,
they cup their hands
with love overflowing.

In the stellar moonlit night,
the nightingale sings
perched on a nogal.

The world whirls,
and their breaths rise
as all breathes well.

Estos amantes
amaron, aman y amarán.

A Note for Noel

O, Noel, a loving man would be so swell
if twice a week you just rang his condo bell.

Tongzhi

Come, my comrade,
be mine and joyful.
We are of the same will
in communion,
yet not yet free
neither in China nor here.

We are patriots
in private and public
sharing the epistemology
of love and codes,
inciting subversion:
our version of love.

La matemática entre nos

If the sum of us is two,
can differences appear?

What's the product then?
Indivisible we live forever.

Numerators and denominators
must be factored in over time, right?

Absolute values appear in the slope of a line.
Are we not facing the real and imaginary together?

Eyes possess eyelids, and screens can go dark.
In dreams we wake, and awakened we perceive.

Tell me the theorem that fuels and keeps us as one.
QEF

Delicate Cycle
for C., Denver-bound

Duchesse satin and embroidered lace dry on delicate cycle.
Snaps whirl and clank with metals and clasps as your mind
in whorl imagines what awaits you. Ah, what the body imagines
and yearns in years! Braille skin rises with lustrous marks,
flickering candles melt for your acolyte lighting and advent.
Wants and needs galore for the woman you adore so afar
from this passage north of gulls and warblers and swallows.
Immense armor of love is yours for this lavender communion.
From one passage to another you ascend and descend, senses
awakened and readied you are for your waltz into open arms.
This is your feast and toast and carnival. Spin, laced as candle
wicks blaze, fueled by your song and homecoming at long last.

Circle of Women

<pre>
                    encircle us
           who   children
        women   adults
     before   elders
   peace   feed us
 offering   manna
radiant   shape us
   again   wise
      homeward   strong
          are   caring &
           we   remember
               summon us
</pre>

Acknowledgments

Grateful acknowledgment is made to several editors and poets who published the following poems, or earlier versions of them, in these publications:

"Anthem" (originally published as "Oh, America, Can You See Us?"). *Critical Insights: The Immigrant Experience*, Maryse Jayasuriya, editor (Grey House Publishing, Inc., 2018), p. 181.

——. *California English: A Quarterly Journal of the California Association of Teachers of English*, vol. 24, no. 3 (Feb. 2019), p. 20.

——. *Critical Storytelling: Multilingual Immigrants in the United States*, Luis Javier Pentón Herrera and Ethan Tính Trinh, editors (Brill Sense, 2021), p. 12.

"Arrangements." *Regeneración Tlacuilolli: UCLA Raza Studies Journal*, vol. 2, no. 1 (2016), pp. 55-56.

"Assessment and Evaluation" (originally published as "Benjamin"). *JoLLE@UGA: Journal of Language & Literacy Education*, vol. 11, no. 1 (2015), pp. 187-188.

"Autobiografía literaria." *Regeneración Tlacuilolli: UCLA Raza Studies Journal*, vol. 2, no. 1 (2016), pp. 67-68.

"Brother's Propaganda." *New Square: The Official Publication of the Sancho Panza Literary Society*, vol. 1, no. 2 (2019), pp. 7-8.

"Endangered Species." *Latino Stuff Review*, vol. 19 (1995), p. 12.

——. *Long River Review*, vol. 19 (2000), p. 38-39.

——. *Flyway: A Literary Review*, vol. 5, no. 3 (2000), pp. 76-77.

"Everyjuan/x" (originally published as "Everyjuan/a"). *California English: A Quarterly Journal of the California Association of Teachers of English 24*, no. 3 (Feb. 2019), p. 21.

———. *Speaking for Ourselves, Vol. 1,* eds. Lorena Germán and Christine Daisy Han (Embracing Equity, 2019), p. 73.

———. *Critical Storytelling: Multilingual Immigrants in the United States,* Luis Javier Pentón Herrera and Ethan Tính Trinh, editors (Brill Sense, 2021), p. 9.

"Galut." *Critical Storytelling: Multilingual Immigrants in the United States,* Luis Javier Pentón Herrera and Ethan Tính Trinh, editors (Brill Sense, 2021), pp. 11-12.

"Henrietta Lacks: HeLa." *English Journal,* vol. 107, no. 1 (2017), p. 77.

"Homeland Insecurity." *Critical Storytelling: Multilingual Immigrants in the United States,* Luis Javier Pentón Herrera and Ethan Tính Trinh, editors (Brill Sense, 2021), p. 11.

"if walt whitman." *Critical Storytelling: Multilingual Immigrants in the United States,* Luis Javier Pentón Herrera and Ethan Tính Trinh, editors (Brill Sense, 2021), pp. 13-14.

"into the fields." *California English: A Quarterly Journal of the California Association of Teachers of English,* vol. 25, no. 3 (Feb. 2020), p. 19.

"las abuelitas." *Flyway: A Literary Review,* vol. 5, no. 3 (2000), pp. 76-78.

———. (originally published as "Viejitas"). *The Thing Itself,* vol. *23* [Our Lady of the Lake University] (1994), p. 14.

"Recuerdo: Say, 'Cheese!'" *California English: A Quarterly Journal of the California   Association of Teachers of English,* vol. 24, no. 3 (Feb. 2019), p. 21.

"Rites for Gregorio Cortez." *El Chisme,* vol. 2, no. 3 [Our Lady of the Lake University] (1993), p. 2.

"Rivers of Languages." *International Perspectives on the Teaching of Literature in Schools: Global Principles and Practices*, Andrew Goodwyn, Cal Durrant, Louann Reid, and Lisa Scherff, editors (Routledge, 2018), p. 112.

"at Sierra de los Mansos" (originally published as "Variation on a Theme by Lucille Clifton"). *Literacy & NCTE Blog*. 2016, April 16.

———. *Pennsylvania Literary Journal*, vol. 10, no. 2 (Summer 2018), pp. 74-75.

"A Teacher Dreams with His Students." *California English: A Quarterly Journal of the California Association of Teachers of English*, vol. 24, no. 3 (Feb. 2019), p. 20.

———. *Critical Storytelling: Multilingual Immigrants in the United States*, Luis Javier Pentón Herrera and Ethan Tính Trinh, editors (Brill Sense, 2021), p. 10.

"terra nostra." *The Texas Observer* (1998, Nov. 6), p. 22.

"Why the Moon is Crescent." *Latino Stuff Review*, vol. 22 (1996), p. 22.

\#

Thank you to my family and friends who have encouraged my writing through the years.

I thank Mario Luis Cardozo Sánchez, Joseph Delgado, Joel R. Garza, Lorena E. Germán, Lisa M. López-Williamson, Joanne Ramirez, Esteban Rodriguez, José Antonio Rodríguez, and Ramón Talavera Franco for their advice and guidance on several of the poems.

A special thanks for the gift of fellowship and amistad to Sean Frederick Forbes. We read the poems closely and pieced and then rearranged them together in the Chihuahuan Desert.

I am grateful for the publishing house and home provided for my poems by FlowerSong Press. Thank you, Edward Vidaurre and your team!

About the Author

R. Joseph Rodríguez was born in Houston, Texas, in 1974. He has published various works as a poet, editor, essayist, literacy advocate, teacher educator, researcher, and translator. His poems have appeared in *California English*, *English Journal, Flyway, New Square, Texas Observer,* and various anthologies. He has held various occupations such as an advisor, busboy, butcher, community organizer, consultant, delicatessen clerk, editor, enumerator, food stocker, instructional coach, interpreter, landscape worker, literacy advocate, research analyst, school bus driver, teacher, and translator. Joseph earned degrees from Kenyon College, the University of Texas at Austin, and the University of Connecticut.

Joseph is the founder of the literacy initiative named Libre con Libros. His recent work involves promoting more community poets in the schools for students and supporting teachers as scribes with their students. He is the recipient of awards and grants from the National Council of Teachers of English and National Endowment for the Humanities.

Joseph lives in Austin and Fredericksburg, Texas. He can be reached via Twitter @escribescribe.